LIVE Your EXCELLENCE:

ACTION GUIDE

Jimmy Casas

ConnectEDD Publishing
Iowa City, Iowa

Praise for *Live Your Excellence*

Just the title alone speaks volumes – *Live Your Excellence: Bring Your Best Self to School Every Day*. When one considers the challenges, obstacles, pressures and demands that accompany so many children as they walk through the entrance doors of their schools every day, on the other side of those doors MUST be adults...educators who strive to "live their excellence" while they simultaneously "bring their best self to school every day." As a follow up to his phenomenal book, *Culturize*, Jimmy Casas digs even deeper with a particular focus on the individual teacher. He offers invaluable advice and strategies on how to consistently bring the best "you" while always maintaining a focus on your "why." *Live Your Excellence: Bring Your Best Self to School Every Day* promises to be a timely asset to all who read it.

Baruti Kafele
Retired Principal, Education Consultant, Author

Shifting from a culture of compliance to one that puts human understanding and grace at the center challenges centuries long top down hierarchical structures; structures that have shut out voices that inform making our educational cultures and systems the best they can be. In *Live Your Excellence*, Jimmy Casas, puts humanness at the center. His highly relatable stories of growth from frustration to understanding and embracing the opportunity to empower the voices that create a positive culture resonate. If we truly value bringing out the best in each other and our students, living our excellence, we must move out of the compliance trap and into cultures of investment.

Pam Gildersleeve-Hernandez
Executive Director, CUE

Jimmy Casas writes as only one who has lived and breathed the work of a true educator can. In *Live Your Excellence*, Casas does it again. He cuts through the noise--the endless initiatives and failed "fixes" for education--and perfectly captures the heart of what truly moves our schools forward: each other

Amy Fast, Ed.D.
High School Principal, Author, and Education Commentator

Live Your Excellence is a beautiful testimony to the power of investing in others and going beyond compliance in the interactions that we have each and every day with both our colleagues and students. If you want to reflect on your work both personally and professionally so that you can grow not only yourself but your school, read this book. Jimmy nails it with *Live Your Excellence.*

Hamish Brewer
Award-Winning Principal and Author

The gold of *Live Your Excellence* isn't in what's *new*, it's in what's *nuanced.* ...Offering nothing new isn't an insult. For educators it is in fact a blessing. The author has an eye for providing new lenses for the work educators are already doing. His insights provide practical application, positive outcomes, and most importantly, paradigm shifts in thinking. He had my book pre-order when I read how he helped empower a principal to shift his mindset and communication around long-standing duties like bus duty, recess duty, lunch duty, and morning duty. Instead of treating it only as a duty, regard it as a relationship opportunity. This is one of the best suggestions I've heard for shifting the thinking around tasks that have often been regarded as an albatross and not an opportunity.

Ken Williams
Author, Speaker, Coach, Status-Quo Disruptor

In *Live Your Excellence: Bring Your Best Self to School Every Day*, Jimmy Casas brings the next step in our growth following what was begun in *Culturize: Every Student. Every Day. Whatever It Takes.* This book is one you will find yourself reading again and again as he reminds us all why we choose to dedicate a large part of ourselves to making a difference in education. Whatever your role is in education, you will find that through this book Casas will help you find the investment-focused mindset and help us all find a way back to living our excellence for our children and ourselves. The reflection prompts that conclude each chapter become guideposts for bringing our best selves to the forefront of our healthier and happier best version of ourselves. A truly great book that deserves a space on your bookshelf, and in your heart.

Denise Murai, School Parent & Community Liaison
HundrED Ambassador, HundrED.org

Jimmy reminds us that we have not set out on this journey to be average. We do the best we can until we know better and then use those learning experiences as opportunities to guide us towards living our excellence. Jimmy's personal stories and experiences will prompt you to pause and self-reflect upon your own practices. He will challenge you to shift your mindset when encountering and responding to difficult situations. Most importantly, you will discover that it's the relationships that we build with our students, colleagues, administrators and families that matter every day! It's the foundation to building a positive school culture where everyone helps, encourages and guides one another towards their personal excellence.

Sharyn Kish
2020 Ohio Teacher of the Year, District 5

In *Live Your Excellence*, Jimmy Casas continues to focus on THE most critical aspect of education, school culture. Blending practical expertise and tips that challenge your thinking as a teacher or principal with heartfelt stories that will leave you yearning for more, "Live Your Excellence" compellingly addresses both the science and the art of education. Jimmy Casas fearlessly tackles the issues in schools no one wants to think or talk about, the undercurrents that form because we're afraid to have the hard conversation. This lack of transparency and authenticity leads us down the road towards negativity, blame, and, ultimately, disenfranchised students and staff. A conventional response to these dangerous undercurrents would be to make people *comply* with "the rules." This book will lead you down another road, one that results in a vibrant, thriving school culture where students and staff *invest* in each other because of an intense commitment to relationships and staying student-centered. A must-read for all educators who desire to have a much greater impact on their students!

Jay Scott
Kansas State Department of Education

Live Your Excellence will have an immediate impact on your school culture. This inspiring read reinforces Jimmy's impact as a thought leader, influencer, and model for our work to transform lives through the art of education. *Live Your Excellence* is a must for those interested in leading from the heart instead of painting inside the lines.

Aaron L. Polansky
Massachusetts Superintendent & Speaker/Author

Live Your Excellence is one of Jimmy Casas's best work! He offers the reader powerful examples of lessons learned from his lengthy career in public education and provides solutions to navigate the challenges of school leadership. Jimmy's humble and vulnerable approach embraces the value of building and cultivating relationships at all levels.

Jerry Almendarez
Superintendent, Santa Ana Unified School District, California

In *Live Your Excellence*, Jimmy Casas takes Culturize deeper so educators can move from a culture of compliance to an investment-based culture. Casas shares how important it is to invest in what is best for students and for you even if it means being vulnerable and sharing mistakes. This book encourages you to consider that learning is more than academics, relationships are not something you can outsource to someone else and why challenging ourselves to do what we ask students to do can motivate us to change. Through personal stories that will touch your heart, scenarios from different perspectives, reflective questions, and strategies for investing in you, Casas demonstrates ways to discover your WHY so you can strive to thrive and live your excellence.

Barbara Bray
Speaker, Podcast Host, Author of *Define Your WHY*

Educators want solid, workable solutions to the challenges they face in leading a new generation of students, and *Live Your Excellence* by Jimmy Casas truly delivers. Through laughter and relevant stories, Jimmy reminds us of the need for personal accountability by admonishing us to "bring your best self to school EVERY day." While that statement seems simple, educators - particularly "seasoned" ones, can easily become complacent if they are not careful. *Live Your Excellence* strikes the perfect balance of encouragement and a necessary "reboot" for every level of school leadership.

Kevin D. Newman, Ed.D.
Superintendent, Manassas City Public Schools

Success in education depends largely on the habits and mindsets we bring to school each day. As such, the books we read have to offer both pragmatic strategies for implementation, and compelling stories for inspiration. Casas delivers both in *Live Your Excellence*. This book is for educators what *The Little Book for Common Sense Investing* is for investors. It is a clear roadmap for investing in children, peers, and ourselves so that cultures of excellence, positivity, and success take hold. Jimmy's love for students and educators is undeniable. Do yourself and your community a favor by taking the time to read this book. We will all be better for it.

Weston Kieschnick
Senior Fellow ICLE, Author, Speaker

LIVE Your EXCELLENCE:

BRING YOUR BEST SELF TO SCHOOL EVERY DAY

ACTION GUIDE

Jimmy Casas

This publication is available at discount pricing when purchased in quantity for educational purposes, promotions, or fundraisers. For inquiries and details, contact the publisher at

info@connecteddpublishing.com

Published by ConnectEDD Publishing LLC
Iowa City, IA
www.connecteddpublishing.com

Cover Design: Kheila Dunkerly

Live Your Excellence: Action Guide/ Jimmy Casas. —1st ed.
Paperback ISBN 978-1-7348908-0-8

Table of Contents

Introduction

This *Action Guide* is a tool to accompany *Live Your Excellence: Bring Your Best Self to School Every Day* by Jimmy Casas. A practical book to help all educators rediscover themselves in order to bring their best self to school every day, *Live Your Excellence* begins with the premise that by cultivating a mindset that centers on investing in students, colleagues, and—most of all—themselves, educators can shift schools away from a culture that runs on compliance, blame, and fear to a culture based on investment and caring. Jimmy shares inspiration, stories, and strategies to help overcome the negative undercurrents that exist in school cultures today and explains how educators of all stripes can embrace an investment-based approach to everything they do, from collaborative leadership, to working with challenging students, to feelings of inadequacy. His insights into navigating the complexities of working in schools is an invaluable resource for all educators who desire—more than anything—to rediscover their own excellence and make a difference. This *Action Guide* is just that: a road map to taking action steps based on the ideas found in *Live Your Excellence*.

Many schools around the world have read Casas's previous book, *Culturize: Every Student. Every Day. Whatever It Takes*. Some of the most rewarding feedback we have received from educators about *Culturize* came from those serving in schools and school districts that conducted whole-faculty book studies based on that book. Our hope is that *Live Your Excellence* will also serve as a book to be used as a professional growth resource in schools and districts everywhere. If you are conducting a book study group, seminar, class, or professional development event based on *Live Your Excellence*, this *Action Guide* will serve as a resource to help you organize your sessions and work with your group. It provides assistance to staff developers, superintendents, principals, team leaders, college professors, and other educational leaders who are working with teachers as they develop their professional skills. In addition, we often facilitate book study workshops ourselves. If you are interested in having someone from our organization help facilitate such a book study, please contact us at:

ConnectEDD Publishing (563) 447-5776 or info@connecteddpublishing.com

Live Your Excellence: Bring Your Best Self to School Every Day is an important book for important people: education professionals. Much like *Culturize*, it is a book that will make you think, but more importantly, make you feel. It reminds readers why they chose to enter this noble profession and why it matters so much to the students, parents, and staff members with whom they interact on a daily basis. This *Action Guide* is intended to take the contents from *Live Your Excellence* and organize them into such a way that provokes discussion, reflection, and--most of all--action. It is written in a way that allows participants to read and understand critical concepts while also applying these in the classrooms and schools in which they serve.

Each part of this *Action Guide* corresponds to several chapters from *Live Your Excellence*. To help you plan and organize your study sessions, the *Action Guide* is divided into the following six sections:

Reflections: These are short thoughts on key sections of the chapter.

Critical Concepts: These are simply bullet-point summaries of the main ideas from each section of the book and are presented here to help you review and focus your thoughts.

Questions to Consider: These questions are designed to reinforce your understanding of critical concepts and will promote constructive conversation among those participating in the study group, workshop, or class.

Writing to Reflect: These reflective journal prompts help you consider what you have read as well as discussions in which you have engaged to independently work through essential issues, recording what you have learned and what you are thinking about in writing.

Team Activities: These activities allow you to further explore concepts and ideas found in *Live Your Excellence* by interacting with others in your study group, workshop, or course.

Putting It to Work: This section provides specific actions for applying what you have learned through your reading as well as work undertaken in the book study back in your own classroom, school, or district.

Thank you for reading *Live Your Excellence: Bring Your Best Self to School Every Day*. Our work as professional educators is so important that we must, indeed, bring our best each and every day. We hope *Live Your Excellence* motivates and inspires educators to do just that and we hope that this companion guide provides a concrete road map for taking the ideas in *Live Your Excellence* and putting them into action. Please reach out to us at **ConnectEDDPublishing (563) 447-5776 or info@connecteddpublishing.com** if we can assist in any way with the work you are doing related to the book and action guide. Please also share your thoughts as well as the work you are doing with us via social media using the hashtag *#LiveYourExcellence.* Thank you for your dedication and commitment to excellence and to the students we serve.

PART I

A Culture of Investment

We can all think of certain times in our lives when we were confronted with the need to change. As lifelong learners, it is important that we not hold so tight to the past that we forget how good the future can be. Clinging to our current practices and policies happens in schools on a regular basis and, although not everything we are currently doing needs to be changed, we can and must do better when we become aware of new and better ways to do so. Building and classroom cultures are negatively impacted when we rely on traditional practices even when we know there are new and better ways to do our work and accomplish our goals--and help our students do the same.

Schools were originally designed to expect and reward a culture of compliance. Students were told what to do and adults were the keepers of the information and the people who determined what would happen and how it would happen. The problem with this model of compliance is that many students did not invest in it since they had no voice in creating it. Students have little or no ownership in this type of culture. Instead of focusing on compliance, we need to create an environment that students are proud to own, one in which they have a voice in how the learning environment looks and feels.

Over the years, somewhere along the way, we may have lost sight of the purpose of education and schooling. Viewing school as an opportunity for continuous growth slowly began to fade away. As we began to compete against other countries and looked to our education system to win this competition, many people thought the correct way to improve was by creating a system in which compliance was rewarded. Still today, we often observe educators focusing more on compliance and control than on patience and understanding. Unfortunately, this is the system we have created in schools for too many years. To change this, we need to ask more questions and stop thinking of students as people we need to control in favor of seeing our students as volunteers who actively choose to invest in their own education as a result of the culture we have created for them in our classrooms and schools.

Many educators worry about losing control in their classroom. Traditionally, we have always been the creator of the rules, and both judge and jury when it comes to student performance. We have worked with many educators who feel it is their role as educators to teach students "life lessons." Although we wholeheartedly endorse the idea of teaching our students about life and preparing them for the future that lies ahead, we also wonder about the potential pitfalls of this mindset when we assume that teaching "life lessons" means insisting that students blindly conform to our expectations. This mindset makes it appear as if we don't care what students as individuals need; instead, we care whether they follow our rules and directions. We need to shift our mindset, ensuring that while it is perfectly acceptable to create cultures in which all students commit to common shared values, it is equally important that we invite and expect that these same students grow, learn, and behave as unique individuals.

Critical Concepts   #LiveYourExcellence

- When we hold students to a standard they cannot reach, we are setting ourselves up for failure and frustration.
- When we fail to make the impact with students that we so desperately hope to, we are at our most vulnerable and most at risk of losing our focus.
- No one goes into this profession to be average. However, we are susceptible to slowly gravitating into average over time if we are not careful.
- Finding our way back to excellence begins with shifting from a culture of compliance to a culture of investment.
- Only by embracing our challenges will we create investment-focused school cultures that reflect our most cherished values.
- In cultures of investment, both students and staff are doing the right thing because in their hearts they believe it is the right thing to do—not because someone else insists they have to do it.

- The foundation of healthy and positive cultures is the way we interact with others and forging relationships based on trust.
- Investment-based educators shift the way they view responsibilities, seeing them not as burdens, but as opportunities.
- Just like we differentiate for academics, we must also differentiate for discipline. What works for one student will not necessarily work for all students--when learning math or learning appropriate behaviors.
- An investment mindset views students as having assets that need to be tapped instead of deficits that must be overcome.
- The best way to ensure that our expectations will be met is to model the behaviors we hope to see.
- A culture of investment is created when everyone knows that their contributions are valued.
- It is important to celebrate our successes together. Validate the work of those involved with a personal and sincere acknowledgement of their work.
- Every moment throughout the school year contains the same promise that the beginning of any new school year does.
- Instead of trying to change the behavior of others, we must try to influence their thinking, so they change their own behavior.
- The way we manage ourselves and the level of sincere investment we exhibit in every interaction we have with every student will eventually determine how they view the adults in their lives.
- Although collaboration can be a productive way of accomplishing goals, professional educators should also have the option of working independently at times.
- We must first take care of ourselves before we can be in the right frame of mind to take care of our students and colleagues. Only by investing in yourself will you have the energy and mindset to truly invest in others.

Questions to Consider   **#LiveYourExcellence**

1. In the Introduction, it appears Ms. Silver is focusing on the compliance of the student to measure the student's success. In what ways do you focus on compliance as an educator?

2. What are some ways you would have worked with Antwan differently than Ms. Silver?

3. What are areas we can focus on as educators to shift from a culture of compliance to a culture of commitment and investment?

4. How can we change our mindset towards students, empowering them to invest in their learning and co-create the learning environment while continuing to have healthy and safe classroom and school environments?

5. We differentiate for student learning styles and academic needs on a daily basis. How can we also begin to differentiate for student behavior?

6. How do you avoid checking-out (losing your drive and passion for your "Why") during the course of a long school year?

7. What are your passions in life? List a few of them below in order of how passionate you are about them. How do your personal passions relate to your work in education? Or do they?

8. How do you currently create a culture in your school or classroom where working collaboratively is valued? Where working independently is valued?

9. Describe a time when responding to a problem the moment you were confronted with it has negatively impacted your performance as an educator?

10. How do you currently ensure that you are caring for yourself at home and at school

Writing to Reflect #LiveYourExcellence

1. Focus on how you are going to make March, April, and May new beginnings for you and your staff and/or students. List the first three steps you will need to take to ensure that you finish the year with just as much energy and enthusiasm as you did to begin the school year. Make sure to include how you will check in on yourself and share with others to help you.

2. Think of a time in your professional or personal life when you were required to do something that you did not necessarily want to do but had to do. Describe the task. Is there any way the person(s) who required you to complete this task could have taken a different approach so that this became something you wanted to do instead of had to do? Can you think of any tasks you are assigning and/or behaviors you are requiring of students or staff that they view as "have to do" rather than "want to do" tasks/behaviors? If so, what can be done to invest them in your expectations?

Team Activities   #LiveYourExcellence

Do You Know Your "Why"?

Purpose of Activity: Identify our purpose in life by looking at different aspects of our character.

1. This activity can be done in small groups.
2. Each person will need to record their responses.
3. Each person will answer the questions below:
   - What makes you come alive?
   - What types of things come easy to you?
   - Where do you exhibit your greatest strengths in your life?
   - What are your core principles in life that drive how you behave? (What is of value to you and helps you measure your level of success?)
   - What is one area of your current skill set that you will work to reinforce? What is an area of refinement, some aspect of your personal and/or professional life about which you will create a goal to improve?
4. After considering the above questions, each individual should craft a succinct, statement called, "My Why." and share with the group.
5. Create an "I Will.." statement, with each participant committing to an action s/he will take moving forward to follow their "why." Purpose of Activity: Identify our purpose in life by looking at different aspects of our character.

Sharing Our Self-Caring   #LiveYourExcellence

Purpose of Activity: Generate ideas and stress the importance of self-care in order to live our excellence each day and better take care of others.

1. Generate 2-3 ideas on self-care strategies you currently use or could use to provide self-care.
2. Share your ideas with group members. Find group members who have one self-care similar to yours.
3. Share ways to track the progress of the specific idea and ways to assist others in obtaining self-care.

Make it a point to share the progress of self-care strategies at the next meeting of the group.

Putting It to Work   #LiveYourExcellence

Score a Goal

Scan the QR Code below to read the article, "16 Actions to Take to Achieve Any Goal." Do these steps apply to educators when it comes to setting personal and/or professional goals? Students?

Identify one goal you have that is related to some aspect of the first four chapters of the book *Live Your Excellence: Bring Your Best Self to School Every Day*. Ideally, make this a SMART (**S**pecific, **M**easurable, **A**ttainable, **R**esults-oriented, and **T**ime bound) goal. Using the 16 actions above as a framework, identify a goal, create an action plan for achieving the goal, and enact the plan.

Notes on Part I - A Culture of Investment   **#LiveYourExcellence**

PART II:

Reaching Students

As educators, we need to focus on the three "Rs" at all times: Relationships, Relationships, Relationships. Not merely social media connections, but true, authentic connections with students, parents, and community members. If we focus on these connections, we can change education. Connections can change the lives of the people with whom we interact each day. Remember back to when you were in school. The people you likely remember most (teachers and friends) are the ones who connected with you the most. Not the people you "liked" or "favorited," but the people with whom you connected on a deeper level. Relationships are the foundation of everything we do as educators.

Every educator has opportunities for growth. One growth area where we often fall short as educators is reflecting on our work, looking at what worked well in addition to what did not. It is important to accept and understand that we are going to struggle at times. Reflection can help us see that the struggles we face and the disappointments we experience in our work are not always as bad as we think and help us to be better prepared for success when similar situations present themselves in the future.

Education also showcases the importance of servant leadership. Each day we work with students, parents, and community members, it is important to remember that we need to give our time and effort to others to set an example, modeling ourselves what we expect of others. Presumably, all of us chose to be in the education profession; indeed, many of us actually felt "called" to enter this noble profession.

Whether we were called to education or simply chose to become educators, the fact remains that we entered what is and always has been a giving profession.

Confidence is one of the foundational aspects of successful teaching and leading. Successful teachers and leaders may not always feel confident but they almost always exude a sense of confidence, not only in themselves, but in those with whom they interact at school as well as in the mission and vision of the school. Confident teachers and administrators tend to make good decisions, trusting in their ability and tendency to make decisions based on what is right for those they serve. This trust in their own decision-making leads, in turn, to others trusting their decision making. Confidence isn't something we are handed or given by others. It is developed over time from the experiences we have, to the habits we acquire, to the practices we employ, and to the mindset we maintain as we approach our work each day.

The greatest gift we can give ourselves and each other is the gift of confidence, the belief that we can do whatever it takes to succeed. The greatest gift we can give the students we serve is also the gift of confidence. Yet, adult self-confidence is different from student self-confidence in one regard. Even when our students have the experiences, habits, practices, and mindset necessary for confidence, this confidence can be fleeting for a variety of reasons. As educators, we need to recognize this and empathize with students to help build and maintain their confidence and belief in themselves.

We often get frustrated when others don't follow our directions. Perhaps we even think they are working against us or they aren't good listeners. When this happens, we need to first look at ourselves and analyze how we delivered the instructions. Instead of blaming others, let's find out how we can be better and more clearly communicate to create less confusion and more clarity.

We've always enjoyed the quote by Mark Victor Hansen, "Each one, reach one. Each one, teach one." Helping build and grow leaders and learners is more than helping them fix problems and find solutions. If you think about it, supplying our future leaders with solutions doesn't help grow them at all. They haven't had to use the problem solving and design process to work through the problem at hand. To cultivate student and staff learners and leaders, it is important for us to coach and help them through these situations. Growth happens through experiences, not by simply implementing solutions created by others.

In life, we often question our impact on society. It's easy to do. In many professions, including education, we don't see the impact our work has on our students for a long time and sometimes, not at all. Not every student passes their classes, not every student comes to school on time daily, and not every student is respectful or appears to care about their own success.

Data such as graduation rates, report cards, discipline, and other measures are important, but do not always reflect the impact we make as educators each day. While our impact in schools can't always be measured, it does not mean that it goes unnoticed by those who we are impacting.

Our consistent and intentional daily efforts as educators to make a difference in the lives of students and staff are critical. We can't focus solely on the here and now and expect to see our impact. The ultimate progress we make over time results from small changes we make to improve in our lives each day. As James Clear says in the book Atomic Habits, "When we make small changes, we don't see immediate results. When you begin to eat the right foods, exercise in small segments, and begin to see yourself as healthy, the results don't show up the next day." Our impact as educators is the same. This impact manifests itself over time. It may be frustrating, at times, when we do not see immediate results of our efforts but trust me: what you are doing today does make a difference; it is worth it.

Critical Concepts   #LiveYourExcellence

- When you are intentional in your interactions with others or give your time to listen to a student or colleague, you have the potential to leave a lasting impact that you may not realize in the moment.
- By investing in relationships with students and colleagues in more meaningful ways, not only can you impact their lives but, in turn, they can change yours.
- It makes us better at what we do when we can empathize with what our students are going through.
- By doing things we fear or struggle with, we can remind ourselves what it feels like to lack confidence.
- When we pause, listen, and understand explanations rather than dismiss what we see as excuses, we may learn that there are bigger issues our students are dealing with and that we, in turn, must deal with.
- When things don't turn out the way you expected, rather than blame others, ask yourself what you might have said or done to contribute to the outcome.
- The ability to self-assess and identify areas where we need to change our practices to improve is critical to success.
- Rather than try to solve others' problems, we should focus on empowering others to become problem solvers themselves.
- When we help a student become a better version of themselves, we, in turn, become a better version of ourselves.
- We must show students that we will do our part whether they do theirs or not. As the adults in the relationship, we must never adopt an "I-will-if-you-will" attitude.

Questions to Consider   #LiveYourExcellence

1. What opportunities do you have each day to connect with students, staff, and parents? Be specific and truthful; look at your day and find all the moments you can build connections with others.

2. What are you grateful for? List five things you are grateful for today or this week.

3. What and how did you give today? List five ways you gave this week, to others or to a specific cause.

4. How do you instill confidence among the people with whom you interact?

5. How do you accept and empathize with unappealing behaviors of students and still help build their confidence levels?

6. From *Live Your Excellence*, list the different ways leaders can help create more problem solvers.

7. What do you do each day to positively impact the lives of students and staff? What are purposeful things you do each day to make a difference?

Writing to Reflect #LiveYourExcellence

1. How do you self-assess when you don't get your desired results? List any steps you consistently take to monitor how you are coming across to others.

2. How confident are you about the work you are doing? How confident are you in the students and/or teachers with whom you work? What helps you to gain self-confidence? What can you do to improve the confidence level within those you serve each day?

Team Activities   #LiveYourExcellence

Communication Champion

Purpose of Activity: To make sure you are providing clear, thoughtful instructions. Use the steps mentioned in the book to provide clear instructions

1. Separate into groups of 3-4.
2. One person in each group is designated as the facilitator for the first session.
3. The facilitator has 2-3 minutes to come up with a topic about which they will provide instructions to the rest of the group (resources needed must be readily accessible).
4. The facilitator then teaches/instructs the group, making sure they utilize the five steps mentioned in *Live Your Excellence* (pp. 53-54).
5. After the "lesson" concludes, group members provide feedback to the facilitator regarding the five steps and their thoughts on the lesson.
6. If time permits, each group member will become the facilitator of a session and receive feedback from others regarding their lesson.

Reflection Will Strengthen Your Teams

Purpose of Activity: To learn the importance of reflection and team building.

1. Each team member needs a sheet of paper.
2. This activity will begin working as individuals, then finish as a team activity.
3. "Identify Who You Are"
   a. Think about the phrase "I am _____."
   b. Fill in the blank on your piece of paper and write down every word that comes to mind. Give yourself some time and create an exhaustive list.
   c. Remember our identities are composed of different aspects of our lives.
4. "Let Hidden Identities Shine"
   a. Which of the ways you identified yourself in the above portion of the activity do you bring to the building/classroom each day?
   b. Which of them do you hide?
   c. How does what is taking place in the building/classroom each day affect the identities you share?

5. "Share Who You Are With Your Team"
   a. Take your identity lists and meet in pairs (or groups of 3-4).
   b. Each person in the group will share what they originally included on their lists and what they omitted.
   c. Each person in the group will share one way they will begin to bring their positive hidden identities to the building/school each day to live their excellence.
6. Share as a large group the similarities and differences among educators in the building.
   a. Collect the information in a Google Doc and determine three ways you will build on the identities to create positive changes in the building.

Putting It to Work

The Things We Say

On page 48 of *Live Your Excellence*, Casas suggests replacing old responses with new language when it comes to the issue of student attendance. What are some other things we have fallen into the habit of saying as educators that can be reframed into more positive and productive language? Here are four examples to ignite your thinking:

"These students can't..."

"She isn't motivated."

"That teacher is so negative."

"Their parents don't care about education."

How can you reframe these statements in a more positive way to turn a deficit into an asset? Spend the next week in your school actively monitoring the language you and your colleagues use when speaking negatively about students or staff. Make it a goal to change your own language as necessary and to respectfully suggest asset-based comments when faced with deficit-based comments among your colleagues.

Notes on Part II - Reaching Students   #LiveYourExcellence

PART III:

Valuing Colleagues

We must take every opportunity available to us to make connections with students. There are times when we are the only ones they can rely on for guidance. It is our job to grow our students and model for them how to make connections with others.

We all want to feel valued and recognized for the great work we do each day. We need to recognize others and their dedication to the profession to build a strong and positive culture in our buildings. When we validate the good work that people do, we are more likely to invest them in the collective mission and vision of the classroom, school, or district.

Support systems are important in education. The job of teaching and leading is hard enough; without the proper support in place for growth and learning, it can become overwhelming.

In the movie *The Pursuit of Happyness*, lead character Chris Gardner tells his son, "If you want something, go get it. Period." Sometimes in education, we get caught admiring what others have instead of visualizing ways we can get the very same thing. Every school and classroom deserve great programs and the best resources. What's best for the best is best for the rest. We can all obtain these great programs and resources as long as we take the appropriate steps to get them.

Gossip is a culture-killer. Plain and simple. It's easy to view gossip as just a normal part of the workplace and something with which we all have to deal. While we agree gossip is present in a number of ways at all schools, it is also our job as educators to do something about it. Ending the negative effects gossip has on culture starts with us as teachers and leaders. We need to model living our excellence by addressing gossip in a direct, yet professional and respectful manner.

As educators, we must manage and monitor our emotions every day. It seems as if the education profession has garnered a great deal of attention--much of it negative--recently, mostly due to the media and social media. As such, educators must work methodically to achieve desired results even in the face of unwarranted external pressures.

Critical Concepts #LiveYourExcellence

- As educators, we can have a huge influence not just on students, but also on colleagues when we invest in them.
- Ultimately, each one of us is responsible for our own morale but each of us also plays a role in determining the morale of the students and staff we work alongside.
- When we dismiss or fail to acknowledge the contributions of students and staff, we miss an opportunity to strengthen the core of our community and to value what people bring to the organization.
- In schools with strong cultures, structured processes are established and adhered to for handling concerns, suggestions, and complaints.
- We cultivate trust when we take the time to personally invest our time in others, and we build confidence when we listen to them and validate their ideas not only by our words, but especially through our actions.
- Labeling some staff members as "rock stars" can work against us, especially if we aim to cultivate a culture in which everyone in the organization feels appreciated.
- When we all intentionally lift each other up, we build a sense of community among the staff and everyone can be celebrated and honored for striving to do what we expect kids to do: the very best they can.
- Until we begin to address gossip in our workplace, we will never reach the standard of excellence most educational organizations aspire to achieve.
- When we gossip, it actually says more about us than the people about whom we are gossiping.
- Supporting others doesn't mean solving their problems but asking questions to better understand their dilemma.
- Managing people to achieve the results we desire requires us to have a clear process for achieving those results.

Questions to Consider   #LiveYourExcellence

1. How do you make others feel valued and recognized? List some things that you already do each week.

2. How do you get others to invest and empower others to find solutions?

3. How can we appropriately recognize "Rock Star" moments at our school? With staff? With students?

4. What will you do this year in your school/classroom to create a "culture of caring" throughout the building?

5. List examples of celebrating school culture and "Rock Star" moments you have seen used by other educators in your school and/or on social media.

6. What support(s) do you have in place in your school and/or district for educator growth and wellness?

7. If you could choose, what additional support(s) would you like to have in place to assist educators? With whom can you connect to begin establishing necessary supports for your building/district?

8. What are your current "great programs" in your school, class, or district? What characteristics do these programs have that make them great? What characteristics can we use from our great programs to grow other programs in our buildings and classrooms?

9. How can educators work together to address the issue of gossiping in schools?

10. Review the 11 steps mentioned in the book (pp. 83-84) for achieving results that you desire as an educator in and in life. Which ones most resonate with you and why? How can you use these in your role as an educator?

11. How can we become better at actively listening, both at work and in our personal lives?

12. How do you ensure you ask good questions when in a conversation?

Writing to Reflect   #LiveYourExcellence

1. **Reflect on the eight ways we can empower others on page 81 of *Live Your Excellence* while working through the below scenario:**

Ron is a principal at a middle school in Indiana. He leads a fairly small middle school, with a student population of 275. One of the school's opportunities for growth consists of improving the daily lunch operations. Ron's middle school has a student-driven idea team that assists with student ideas to help improve the school.

A student at Ron's school sent him an email at approximately 3:30 p.m. on a Monday. The student had some suggestions about improving the school lunch and the lines for lunch that were constantly backed up. The student shared with Ron that he had worked with 7th grade language arts teacher Ms. Winters for at least three months to help develop a plan to improve the lunch operations.

Ron replied back to the student via email on Thursday afternoon. Ron thanked the student for reaching out to him with his ideas. He also let the student know that he would contact Ms. Winters to have a conversation with her about the ideas. Ron emailed Ms. Winters three weeks later regarding the original email the student had sent.

Ron also scheduled a meeting a week later with Ms. Winters, the student, the cafeteria supervisor, and three teacher leaders in the building. Ron opened the meeting by asking everyone how they thought the cafeteria could be improved. He then told the group how he would handle changing the cafeteria for the better.

Ron made a few changes as he tried to improve the cafeteria for students, but he didn't use anyone's suggestions from the meeting he convened, not even those of the student who originally reached out to him.

How well did Ron perform in the scenario above? Address the following questions in your response:

- What did Ron do well?
- Where could Ron have done better?
- How would you have celebrated the student and Ms. Winters?

2. **Refer to the twelve ways to address gossip in Live Your Excellence (pp. 76-77) to work through the exercise below:**

Mark approached Carol in the hallway outside her classroom before the day began. Mark told Carol a story from the day before when he and Bart disagreed about an assessment question in their department meeting.

Mark said to Carol, "Bart got in my face a little bit about one of our assessment questions for the Unit 2 test in Biology. He said in front of everyone that the question needed more substance. Substance? I wonder if he needed substance when he asked Janelle out for a date during our building Happy Hour last week. Did you know he did that?"

Carol replied, "Oh my Gosh! Really? That is unreal!"

Mark continued, "Bart has no idea what we should assess on the Unit 2 test. He did awful on this topic when he was in college. He barely passed the class. I've heard students say he doesn't know what he's doing on Unit 2."

Mark stormed off, but not before saying, "I don't care who you share this information with Carol. Bart needs to get in the game!"

Carol was shocked. She sees Janet as she walks into the staff lounge. Carol says to Janet, "You won't believe what I just heard about Bart and Janelle."

Reflect on the scenario above and address the following:

*   Discuss and list how some or all of the twelve ways to address gossip from *Live Your Excellence* should be applied in the above scenario.
*   How could each person have responded differently to achieve a better outcome for all: Mark? Carol? Janet?

Team Activities   #LiveYourExcellence

Summarize This!

Purpose of Activity: Participants hear a story and use skills learned to summarize the story.

1. Organize participants into pairs.
2. Take five minutes to individually think about a school or current event topic you can share with a partner.
3. Designate who will be the summarizer.
4. The other person shares a story while the summarizer must use skills learned above to summarize the story they hear.
5. Switch roles after the first summarizer finishes.
6. Each person provides feedback on their partner's summaries.

Top Traits

Purpose of Activity: List and Define the qualities of great programs and create steps to build on existing programs.

1. On page 74, Casas describes five processes used to create successful programs. In this activity, individual participants will list the qualities that they believe compose the great programs in their building/classroom and/or great programs they know about in different schools. Try to come up with as many "great traits" as possible.
2. Next, each individual will share their list with a partner and combine their list into a streamlined list of ten traits.
3. Each group of two will pair with another group to create another revised list of ten traits of a great program. Each group will need a recorder and facilitator to document the information and share their list when they meet as a whole group.
4. Finally, the entire group will come together and the facilitator will ask each group to share their lists. The entire group will then create a list of Top Traits of great programs.
5. While the entire group is still together, ask the group to share a list of current programs in the building or individual classrooms that currently exist. Facilitator will record the programs shared by the group.

6. Divide the entire team into smaller groups, asking each group to take one of the programs shared.

7. Using the five processes the author shared on page 74 and the list of Top Traits of great programs created by the entire group, record how the specific program for your group already has the qualities listed. Next, record the qualities the program is lacking.

8. As a group, create a list of three steps that can be taken to build on the positive aspects of the program and three steps to take to for opportunities for growth of the program.

Entire group will come together and share their steps for their specific programs. Decide how to take next steps to help the programs become even better? Set a goal for creating/leading a new program needed in the school to help staff and students live their excellence.

Putting It to Work   #LiveYourExcellence

The "I's" Have It

On pages 85-87 of *Live Your Excellence,* Casas shares eight reminders for keeping your eyes on an investment focus in your role as an educator, with each reminder beginning with the letter "I." Review these eight "I's." Choose just one of the "I's" to focus on during your work with a colleague in the next week. Create a plan in advance and set it into action with a staff member you supervise or serve alongside. Record your impressions of how it went and the extent to which it made a difference. Share at the next meeting of the group.

Got Questions?

Scan the QR code below and read the article, "The One Conversational Tool That Will Make You Better at Absolutely Everything." What are the keys to asking great questions? How can you use effective questioning techniques to improve as an educator? Monitor a professional conversation you have in the next week with a parent, student, or colleague. Make a point to ask questions with a purpose following guidelines in the article. Did your questioning yield better results?

Notes on Part III - Valuing Colleagues   **#LiveYourExcellence**

PART IV:

Developing Leadership

Communication can make or break us as educators. It is important to cultivate the communication skills that allow for critical conversations with others. In order for us to create a culture with a foundation based on modeling and truthfulness, we need to find it among ourselves to communicate with others, even when that requires us to engage in difficult conversations.

No one is perfect, not even the very finest educators we know. In education, we encounter so many decisions we must make each day that we are bound to slip-up from time to time. The real question to ask and consider is when we do make a mistake, how do we recover? If we can recognize that we made a mistake and apologize when we need to, we build a culture in our classrooms and buildings that making mistakes is OK and that acknowledging we made a mistake is the right thing to do. We must always model the behaviors we expect from others.

We believe that every educator wants to bring their best every day. No one wakes up wanting to be average. Everyone is trying the best they can at any particular moment in time. But there are times we lose focus on living our excellence. When that happens, we need to get back to our "why" and focus on our priorities.

We believe that one of the most rewarding aspects of collaboration is being able to hear other voices when we work through difficult or less-than-ideal situations. Regardless of the specific situation, hearing others voices on the matter provides us with an opportunity to consider different perspectives and philosophies. Working with staff, students, or community members who constantly complain is but one example of the many unpleasant situations we all deal with. But, there are ways to work through these complaints (and work with these complainers) that allow us to help get the complainers to invest in their own problems and, ultimately, help strengthen our cultures.

As it says in the book, credibility is the key to getting others to trust us and invest in us and the overall work we do. For leaders, credibility provides the foundation for a culture of change, commitment, and investment. Addressing underperformance is difficult. Coaching those who underperform is also difficult. However, both are critical in terms of maintaining our credibility and improving our schools. What we must remember as educators and leaders is that if we do not address underperformance, we are unwittingly accepting it as part of our culture. Positive, productive, growth-mindset cultures never accept underperformance. No one enjoys addressing underperformance, but truly excellent educators do it anyway.

A lack of established processes to address the problems we face also contributes to poor decision making. As educators, we must follow processes and protocols to avoid common mistakes that inevitably arise over the course of a school year.

At times, we may get defensive when people question how we handle different situations. Human nature has us put up walls at times to protect ourselves, including when working with difficult parents. To avoid this natural tendency, we must see parents as advocates not only for their kids, but also for our work. All parents want their children to be successful at school. No one wants their own offspring to fail. We need to remember this when we are working with parents in emotionally-charged situations. We must focus on de-escalating situations and remembering that parents are our partners and advocates in the process.

You cannot fake caring about others. We need to genuinely care about others to create a culture of trust and respect. There are some students in every school to visit who feel that some educators at their school do not genuinely care about them. There are also educators who feel the same about their administrators. We must work intentionally to create a culture of caring in our schools and modeling what genuine caring looks like.

Critical Concepts #LiveYourExcellence

- Most students and staff members will respect and appreciate us more when we keep difficult conversations real and recognize our own shortcomings, rather than pretend we have all of the answers.
- As leaders, we will make mistakes. However, we must not allow this to produce a kind of tentative thinking on our part, which could cause us to hesitate, over-think, and second-guess ourselves.
- When we struggle, we need purpose more than we need happiness. Deeply fulfilled people seem to know their purpose in life.
- Everyone in an organization has the capacity to lead—though whether we choose to lead is a different issue.
- Leadership requires a willingness to invest a tremendous amount of personal time to grow and develop the abundance of skills that we currently lack—it's not something that any one of us is born with.
- Credibility is what allows us to influence others in a positive way. Credible leaders do what they say they are going to do.
- Underperformance of students and staff members is going to be an issue, but failing to address underperformance has the potential to become an even bigger one.
- Both students and staff want to know that we care about them. Ironically, one way we show that we care is by addressing underperformance.
- Every student and staff member deserves to be treated fairly and to believe that we care about them.
- Education is a responsibility and obligation that should be shared by the school, students, a child's guardians, and the community.
- Parents have a right to show up for their children, and we should expect them to advocate for them.
- When people feel valued and cared for, their personal excellence will rise above their moments of disappointment.

Questions to Consider   **#LiveYourExcellence**

1. Do you fear or avoid conversations that elicit emotional responses? If so, why? What is the worst thing you feel can happen from these types of conversations? If you don't mind those conversations and engage in them, why is it easier for you to do this?

2. List two experiences in your life that were catalysts for your future success. How have these experiences shaped you as an educator?

3. What are four ways to manage complainers?

4. How do we find the right things to say in difficult times?

5. What are your processes for addressing underperformance either in the classroom, school, or both?

6. On pages 113-115 of *Live Your Excellence*, Casas lists twelve things leaders should stop doing. Which of these areas would you choose to work on immediately?

7. How do you create clear expectations for staff and students? How do you know they are clear?

8. When you ask for feedback from those you lead, what steps do you take to communicate back to the staff about your follow up to the feedback you received?

9. What steps can you take to be a "doer" and not a critic?

10. What are effective strategies you use and/or have seen others use when working successfully with parents? Why do they work?

11. How do you and others in your school exhibit genuine caring for students and each other? Are there ways we can improve in this area?

12. What type of support programs do you have in place to address students' social/emotional needs? What can you do differently or additionally?

13. Do you show gratitude every day when you walk into the building/classroom? If so, how do you do it? If not, are there things you can start doing to express gratitude openly?

Writing to Reflect   #LiveYourExcellence

1. I believe that every excellent teacher is a leader and every excellent leader is a teacher. Serving as an educator means serving as a leader, regardless of your role in education. Reflect on the list of leadership traits below:

Servant	Courageous	Sense of Humor	Passionate	Caring
Assertive	Visionary	Communicator	Empathetic	Trustworthy
Honest	Charismatic	Inspiring	Delegator	Confident

What are three characteristics above that you possess or already do well as an educator? How did these three traits become strengths of yours? What are three characteristics from the list which you can improve upon?

2. We cannot choose the students who come to our school. We cannot always choose with whom we work in our schools. In fact, there are many things related to the work we do that are beyond our control. However, one thing we can choose is our attitude and the way we approach our work each and every day. Think of someone you know who typically has a good attitude. What about them makes you think that? Think of someone you know who typically has a lousy attitude. What about them makes you think that?

- When you think of the person with a bad attitude, what things or people does that person usually point to as the reason they are in a bad mood?
- What factors influence your attitude each day, causing shifts from good to bad when it comes to your own attitude?
- What influences our attitudes?
- Must you have a bad attitude if things aren't going your way or do you think it's possible to have a good attitude even when bad stuff is happening? Why?
- Are there things in your life you'd like to change to help you have a more positive attitude?
- If negative stuff is happening to you, are there things you can do to keep your outlook positive?

Discuss the power of a positive attitude and what we can do as educators to maintain a positive attitude ourselves and instill it within others:

Team Activities   **#LiveYourExcellence**

What Makes Me Great?

Purpose of Activity: Find out from others what makes you great.

1. Work in groups of 3-5. It is important that members of the group know each other.
2. On a sheet of paper, write your name at the top and the questions, "What makes me great? What are the traits I have that help me be a great leader and educator?"
3. Each group member passes the paper to their right.
4. Each group member writes down the best traits of the person whose name is at the top of the page.
5. Continue to pass the paper to the right until you receive your own paper.
6. Each person can share their specific traits in the group.
7. How will you build on your best traits? What traits are missing that you will try to acquire or work on? Who can help you with these?

The Complain Game

Purpose of Activity: To help us handle complaints from staff, students, and/or parents.

Utilize the four ways to manage (pp. 99-100 in *Live Your Excellence*) complainers to navigate the scenarios below:

1. Work with a partner (this can be done in groups of 4 also for more feedback).
2. One person will be the complainer; the other will be a teacher/administrator "listener."
3. Use the complaints below (or other complaints your specific department, school, or district may encounter) and use the four steps mentioned in the book to work through each of these scenarios:

- "Why do I have a duty during the day when others on the staff don't have to do anything? To me, that isn't fair."
- "I don't like how things are going for my son in his teacher's class. I want him moved to a different class and would like his grade to be an 'A' as he starts with the new teacher."
- "You scheduled the school play on a night I can't attend. I would like the date for the play moved so I can attend with my family."

Rate My Traits   #LiveYourExcellence

Purpose of Activity: Participants will get feedback from their peers on what traits they have and how to improve perceived areas of need.

1. Each participant will need a piece of paper.
2. Sit in a group of at least 4 people.
3. Draw a tic-tac-toe board on your paper.
4. In the middle square, write down a characteristic you feel you do well on the top half of the block.
5. In the same square, write down a characteristic you feel you could improve upon.
6. Pass your paper clockwise to a person at your table.
7. Each participant will write down an idea or thought on how to improve each characteristic.

Pass the papers around until you receive your own paper.

Putting It to Work #LiveYourExcellence

My Credibility Score

List all seven areas that credible leaders do (pp. 105-106 of *Live Your Excellence*) on a piece of paper. Leave space below each one to create a scale. Create a Likert scale of 1-5 under each area, with 1 representing "Do it often" and 5 representing "Don't do it at all."

Possible questions to ask (feel free to include your own):

- Do I make excuses?
- Have you heard me make excuses or feel I make excuses why I or we can't do something?
- Do I celebrate others?
- Do you feel celebrated when you do something well?
- Do I act more like a learner or a knower?
- How well do I accept feedback from others?
- How truthful do you feel I am?
- Do I own my data?
- Rate me on how I handle difficult conversations

Present the questions to students or colleagues with whom you interact daily and have them complete a Likert scale with you in mind based on the questions above. Collect the feedback from others and determine what areas you are going to focus on for improvement. Establish a timeline for your goal and follow up with students/colleagues, asking if they have noticed improvement over the time period.

Notes on Part IV - Developing Leadership   **#LiveYourExcellence**

BRING YOUR BEST SELF TO SCHOOL EVERY DAY:

17 Keys for Living Your Excellence as an Educator

Part One: A Culture of Investment

The Compliance Trap: *When we focus on telling people what to do, we unintentionally create a culture of compliance. Don't tell others what to do, show them.*

Where to Start with a Culture of Investment: *Communicate expectations clearly and then model the standard of excellence you want others to emulate.*

What an Investment Mentality Entails: *Processes, structures, and frameworks are critical in order to create a system of excellence. Systems are imperative because they promote equity for all.*

Invest in Yourself: *Be sure to look after your own personal needs so that you are also in the right frame of mind to take care of the needs of your colleagues and students.*

Part Two: Reaching Students

So Glad You Are Here Today: *Relationships are not something to outsource to someone else. Begin to see every interaction with a student or colleague as an opportunity to shine your excellence on them.*

Remembering What It's Like: *We should not ask others to do what we are not willing to do ourselves first.*

Investing by Self-Assessment: *Rather than blaming others when you do not get the results you hoped for, start by looking within to see what you may have contributed to the outcome.*

Is It Worth It?: *When we quit on a student, they know it and you know it. When we refuse to give up, then we can have hope and faith that we left a positive mark on that student.*

Part Three: Valuing Colleagues

The Influence of Investment: *One of the most precious gifts we can give to others is the gift of time. Our influence is even greater when we invest in our students and colleagues in a kind and caring way that supports their success.*

Every Contribution, Every Day: *Regardless of our position or title in school, all of us play a role in determining the morale of those we work alongside.*

When Educators Gossip: *When we fail to address gossip in our workplace, we fall short of the standard of excellence we aspire to achieve, expect, and even advertise.*

Results: *Supporting others doesn't mean always solving their problems. Sometimes we need to invest more time asking questions in order for them to come up with ideas to solve their own issues and build capacity.*

Sustaining an Investment Outlook: *There will always be challenges in our work. View yourself as a learner first and understand you won't always get it right the first time. Own it, apologize, and forgive yourself.*

Part Four: Developing Leadership

The Courage to Act and the Courage to Ask: *Don't pretend to have all the answers. Accept there will be days when you don't know what to do. In these moments ask for help. We are all a work in progress.*

What It Takes to Lead: *Effective leaders have an acute self-awareness and an ability to draw on the right skill or resource in any given moment. This requires a willingness to invest the time necessary to grow and develop the same skills that we may be lacking.*

Navigating Difficult Conversations: *We cannot accept substandard performances by our students, but more importantly, we cannot accept substandard performances by ourselves. We must have the courage to address underperformance professionally, respectfully, and honestly.*

Invest in Excellence for Everyone: *Commit to simply trying to better yourself in every aspect of your life and believe that you can inspire others to new heights as well...to live their excellence every day!*

References and Resources

Casas, J. (2017). *Culturize: every student, every day, whatever it takes*. San Diego, CA: Dave Burgess Consulting, Incorporated.

Casas, J., & Zoul, J. (2018). *Stop. Right. Now.: the 39 stops to making schools better*. San Diego, CA: Dave Burgess Consulting, Incorporated.

Casas, J. (2020). *Live Your Excellence bring your best self to school every day; bring your best self to school every day*. San Diego, CA: Dave Burgess Consulting, Incorporated.

Clear, J. (2018). *Atomic habits: tiny changes, remarkable results: an easy & proven way to build good habits & break bad ones*. New York: Avery, an imprint of Penguin Random House.

Patel, D. (2018, August 27). 16 Actions to Take to Achieve Any Goal. Retrieved from https://www.entrepreneur.com/article/318347

Snow, S. (2013, May 10). The One Conversational Tool That Will Make You Better At Absolutely Everything. Retreived from https://www.fastcompany.com/3003945/one-conversationaltool-will-make-you-better-absolutely-everything

More Books
by Jimmy Casas:

Live Your Excellence: Bring Your Best Self to School Every Day by Jimmy Casas

Culturize: Every Student. Every Day. Whatever It Takes. By Jimmy Casas

What Connected Educators Do Differently by Todd Whitaker, Jeffrey Zoul, and Jimmy Casas

Start. Right. Now. Teach and Lead for Excellence by Todd Whitaker, Jeffrey Zoul, and Jimmy Casas

Stop. Right. Now. The 39 Stops to Making Schools Better by Jimmy Casas and Jeffrey Zoul

About The Author

Jimmy Casas served twenty-two years as a school leader. He is a best-selling author, speaker, leadership coach, and a state and national award-winning principal. Under Jimmy's leadership, Bettendorf High School was named one of the best high schools in the country three times by Newsweek and U.S. News and World Report.

Jimmy was named the 2012 Iowa Principal of the Year and was runner-up NASSP 2013 National Principal of the Year. In 2014, Jimmy was invited to the White House to speak on the Future Ready Pledge. Finally, in 2015, he received the Bammy Award for the National Principal of the Year. Jimmy is the author of several books, including *What Connected Educators Do Differently, Start. Right. Now. – Teach and Lead for Excellence, Culturize: Every Student. Every Day. Whatever It Takes., Stop. Right. Now. 39 Stops to Making Schools Better,* and *Live Your Excellence: Bring Your Best Self to School Every Day.*

Jimmy currently serves as an adjunct professor for Drake University, teaching courses in educational leadership. Finally, he is the owner and CEO of J Casas & Associates, an educational leadership company aimed at providing world-class professional learning services for educators across the country.

About ConnectEDD

Since 2015, ConnectEDD has worked to transform education by empowering educators to become better-equipped to teach, learn, and lead. What started as a small company designed to provide professional learning events for educators has grown to include a variety of services to help teachers and administrators address essential challenges. ConnectEDD offers instructional and leadership coaching, professional development workshops focusing on a variety of educational topics, a roster of nationally-recognized educator associates who possess hands-on knowledge and experience, educational conferences custom-designed to meet the specific needs of schools, districts, and state/national organizations, and ongoing, personalized support, both virtually and onsite. In 2020, ConnectEDD expanded to include publishing services designed to provide busy educators with books and resources consisting of practical information on a wide variety of teaching, learning, and leadership topics. Please visit us online at connecteddpublishing.com or contact us at:

info@connecteddpublishing.com

Made in the USA
Monee, IL
05 February 2021